THE BRILLIANT DEEP

REBUILDING THE WORLD'S CORAL REEFS

THE STORY OF KEN NEDIMYER AND THE
CORAL RESTORATION FOUNDATION

KATE MESSNER   **MATTHEW FORSYTHE**

chronicle books·san francisco

It starts with one.

One night, after a full moon,
the corals begin to spawn—
releasing first one, then millions
of tiny lives—until the waters swirl
like a snow globe.

Some become food for hungry fish.

Some are washed into the deep sea.

Some drift in the currents until they come
to rest, not too deep, on the ocean floor.

If one is lucky, it lands in a
place where it can grow.

This one will begin a coral reef.

KEN NEDIMYER grew up near Florida's Kennedy Space Center, watching America race toward the moon.

Before men took off in rockets, Ken's father worked at NASA as an engineer.

Ken watched his father's team send unmanned
rockets—Little Joe, Redstone, Atlas—toward the stars.
Men followed—Alan Shepard, John Glenn.

It seemed like just about anything might
be possible if you set your mind to it.

But Ken's dreams weren't in the stars.

He loved the ocean.

He watched TV shows about underwater
explorer Jacques Cousteau.

He visited the beach whenever he could,
    swimming far out to a world of angelfish and sea stars.

The reefs of the Florida Keys teemed with life.

They painted the ocean floor fire red and murky gold.
How could the reefs grow so large?
What made all the different colors and shapes?
How could such tiny creatures build such elaborate homes of rock?

Ken learned to scuba dive and began collecting fish to keep and study at home. At one point, he had thirty aquariums in his bedroom, all bursting with life.

Ken's favorite place was always out on the reef . . .
until things began to change.

ONE SUMMER, hotter than the rest,
Ken noticed the corals were losing their color,
and there weren't as many fish.

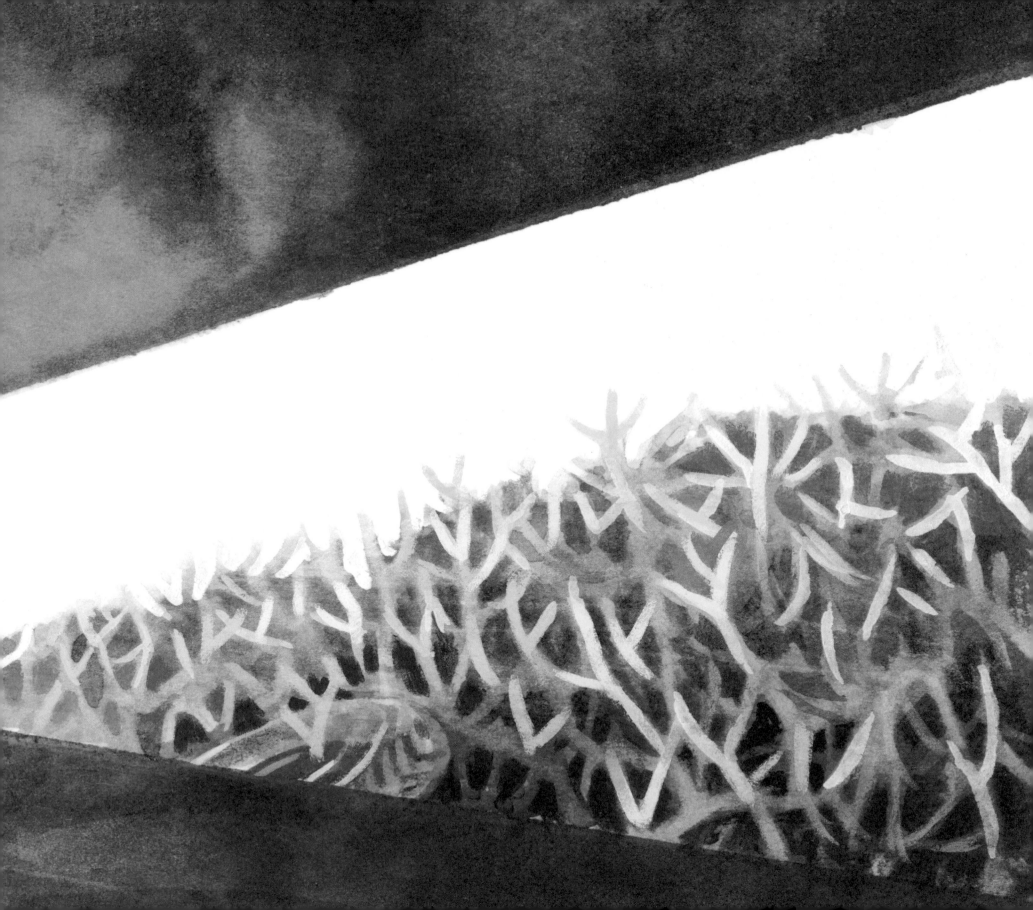

The sea urchins had started to die. They are the gardeners of the reef, tiny groundskeepers who control the algae. But Ken didn't know that at the time.

Even scientists didn't understand what an important role the sea urchins played until they were gone.

Ken watched his favorite place in the
world begin to fade away.

The reefs were dying, and it seemed like
there was nothing he could do to save them.

But one day, that changed.
Ken was all grown up, operating a live
rock farm in the Florida Keys.

Live rocks aren't really alive;
they're rocks covered with algae,
mollusks, sponges, and other
invertebrates. They're used in saltwater
aquariums as decoration and to filter
waste from the water, turning poisons
like ammonia and nitrates into
harmless compounds. This makes
the water safer and healthier
for everything that lives in it.

And growing them is really just a matter of patience . . . placing rows of bare rocks on the ocean floor and waiting for the marine life to move in.

On one moonlit night, a nearby coral colony spawned, and a few of those delicate lives found their way to Ken's rocks. They grew into staghorn corals.

Staghorn corals are protected—illegal to take from the ocean floor. But the law says if a coral colony grows on a live rock farm, the owner can keep it.

Ken could have sold his specimens to someone with a saltwater aquarium. But instead, he and his daughter had an idea. As the corals grew, they cut off pieces and attached those pieces to other rocks. They discovered they could use those first colonies to grow more and more corals.

What would happen if someone grew a coral colony and then
tried to plant it on a dying reef? Would it grow? Could that colony help
rebuild the reefs Ken loved? Could a reef come back to life?

Ken made plans to go to the reef,
where he'd loved diving as a kid, to find out.

He selected his coral colonies.

He loaded his scuba gear and supplies . . .

and set out for the reef.

One hopeful dive . . .

One optimistic experiment . . .

Six small coral colonies—each one the size of a hand with the fingers stretched—glued onto a limestone surface where a reef had once flourished and was now bleached and barren.

Would they grow?

Ken and his friends came back to check on the coral colonies
again and again. Each month, they had grown larger. It was too soon to say
if the reef would fully recover, if the fish would return.

But it was a beginning.

Ken started a group called the Coral Restoration Foundation—
a small army of volunteers on a mission to restore the reefs. They hang bits of
coral on special underwater trees and lines where the corals can grow.

When the corals are
large enough, these
farm-raised colonies are
loaded onto boats with
volunteers, dive equipment,
and tools.

Then, it's out to a new home.
One the corals will help to build.

Volunteers take great care with this homecoming.
They search for just the right spot—a place where each
coral colony can hold on once it's grown enough to attach
to the reef on its own. Divers scrape off any algae.
They use chipping hammers, scraping and banging
to get the surface even and smooth.

Then, with a careful dab of epoxy—just the size of a Hershey's Kiss—volunteers attach the coral colonies. Piece by piece, arm by arm. Hoping they will grow on their own.

Today, the transplants are not only surviving, but also reproducing. Ken's group has planted tens of thousands of coral colonies on reefs in the Florida Keys. And now, he's working with other countries, teaching people how to grow corals of their own to save the reefs they love, too.

TONIGHT, the moon will be full and bright.
The corals may spawn, and if one tiny life lands in
just the right spot, another new colony will grow.

And then another.

And another.

And another.

It starts with one.

WHAT HAPPENED TO THE CORAL REEFS?

There's no question that the world's coral reefs are dying at an alarming rate. Today, there is less than half as much coral cover in the Caribbean as there was in the 1970s. On some reefs, just a small fraction of the corals remain alive. The reasons are complicated. Scientists believe that changing ocean temperatures, disease, boating, and overfishing have all contributed to the problem.

Ken and his team are part of the solution, especially as their ideas and techniques spread to other countries. Other scientists think protecting parrotfish and sea urchins might help save the reefs, since these animals eat the algae that can overwhelm corals if it's not kept in check. There's also hope that corals might be bred to withstand higher ocean temperatures in the future.

HOW CAN KIDS HELP?

The Coral Restoration Foundation has hundreds of volunteers who help to farm and transplant corals. They practice attaching dead corals to a table with Play-Doh to get ready for the big day. They are carefully trained above water before they dive to work on the reef, because when they're actually underwater, it's much harder to talk and learn.

You can help the foundation's volunteers with their efforts, even if you don't know how to scuba dive.

The Coral Restoration Foundation has an Adopt-a-Coral program to help pay for its projects. A single coral fragment costs about a hundred dollars to grow and plant. Families and classrooms can plant a coral colony—or even adopt a whole tree in the nursery—by making donations through the foundation's website: www.coralrestoration.org/adopt-a-coral/

READ MORE

Chin, Jason. *Coral Reefs*. New York: Flash Point, 2011.
Gibbons, Gail. *Coral Reefs*. New York: Holiday House, 2010.
Simon, Seymour. *Coral Reefs*. New York: HarperCollins, 2013.

EXPLORE ONLINE

Organizations:

Coral Restoration Foundation
www.coralrestoration.org

Nature Conservancy Coral Restoration Program
www.nature.org/ourinitiatives/regions/northamerica/unitedstates/
florida/howwework/stimulating-coral-restoration.xml

National Oceanic and Atmospheric Administration (NOAA)
Habitat Restoration: Coral Reefs
www.habitat.noaa.gov/restoration/approaches/corals.html

Articles:

Gambino, Megan. "A Coral Reef's Mass Spawning."
Smithsonian Magazine, December 2009.
www.smithsonianmag.com/arts-culture/a-coral-reefs-
mass-spawning-147635608/

Murphy, Kara. "Coral Spawning: A Rare Natural Wonder."
Australian Geographic, December 15, 2011.
www.australiangeographic.com.au/topics/wildlife/2011/12/
coral-spawning-a-rare-natural-wonder/

CORAL REEF VOCABULARY

corals: Marine invertebrates that usually live in colonies made up of identical individual organisms, known as polyps.

exoskeleton: A hard external skeleton that covers the body of some invertebrates. Coral polyps secrete a substance called calcium carbonate, which forms exoskeletons.

polyp: A single coral organism within a colony.

coral reef: A community of living creatures living on and around a rocky undersea formation created by the exoskeletons of corals.

gametes: Egg and sperm cells released when corals spawn. When these combine, they form embryos, which develop into larvae and, under the right conditions, grow into new coral colonies.

spawn: The synchronized release of millions of gametes from coral polyps of the same species.

For Abby and Will, with love —KM

For Lauren —MF

Library of Congress Cataloging-in-Publication Data:
Names: Messner, Kate, author. | Forsythe, Matthew, 1976- illustrator.
Title: The brilliant deep : rebuilding the world's coral reefs : the story of
Ken Nedimyer and the Coral Restoration Foundation / by Kate Messner ;
illustrated by Matthew Forsythe.
Description: San Francisco, California : Chronicle Books, 2018. | Audience:
Age 5 to 8. | Audience: K to Grade 3.
Identifiers: LCCN 2016010977 | ISBN 9781452133508 (alk. paper)
Subjects: LCSH: Coral reef conservation—Juvenile literature. | Nedimyer,
Ken—Juvenile literature. | Coral Restoration Foundation—Juvenile
literature.
Classification: LCC QH75 .M44 2018 | DDC 333.95/53153—dc23 LC
record available at https://lccn.loc.gov/2016010977

Manufactured in China.

MIX
Paper from
responsible sources
FSC
www.fsc.org   FSC™ C104723

Design by Amelia May Mack.
Typeset in Nobel and Lulo.

10 9 8 7 6 5 4 3 2 1

Chronicle Books LLC
680 Second Street
San Francisco, California 94107
www.chroniclekids.com

Top: Ken Nedimyer
photo credit: Denise Nedimyer

Bottom: A restored coral reef with two-year-old staghorn coral
photo credit: Ken Nedimyer